The Product is YOU!

A Practical Guide to Career Management

Raymond T. Hoppenjans

DEDICATION

To my family, my greatest "accomplishment" in life.

Problem: Find a girl who could put up with me

Action: Marry her

Result: Two of my proudest "accomplishments" and a life too blessed for one man to live

Table of Contents

Figures

ACKNOWLEDGMENTS

I had no intention of writing a book. I was content to coach people and offer sage advice. I'm qualified to categorize my advice as "sage" by virtue of the color of my hair and the number of aches and pains that come from many years of life experience. If my friend Buzz Woeckener hadn't sought out such "sage" advice and recommended that I write a book, I never would have done it. Thank you Buzz.

I would also like to acknowledge Chris Metcalf for helping me think through the components of my process and for providing early edits and many improvements. Thank you Chris.

Thanks to my dear friend Dr. Robert (Bob) Bober for reading the book from multiple perspectives and providing advice for improvement from each.

Thanks to my very good friend Joe Michael for his edits and suggestions for future improvements.

I want to thank my wife Jeanne for reviewing this book multiple times and for listening to me talk about it for months.

And finally, I want to thank my daughters, Kelly and Katie. Without them this book would be littered with grammar and spelling errors.

Introduction

A few years ago I was in a mentoring session with a colleague and friend of mine. He wanted to discuss his career and was looking for advice. Specifically, he wanted to know how to figure out which jobs were best suited for him, when he should pursue a job and how to prepare to give himself the best possible chance of winning the job. We met several times over the next few months. I took him through a process that helped him organize his thoughts in a way that allowed him to see his career as a progression of steps leading to his goal. We discussed how to convert the steps into a plan, talked about the specific actions he could take to improve his odds of getting interviews, and, finally, we outlined how to implement the plan.

One day during one of our sessions, my friend looked at me and said, "This process is really good. It's practical and puts everything into a clear set of actions for me to execute. I can see how I can use this in other parts of my life. You should write a book about this!" Honestly, I had never considered writing a book about anything in my life. I'm not a writer, as you will no doubt agree, after you read this book. But after some prodding from my friend, I decided he was right. The process was good and it could help a lot of people struggling with the same questions with which he had wrestled. So I decided to write the book. But what is the process, and how did I come up with it?

I applied for a job with IBM at the suggestion of my friend Dick. You see, I was playing offensive guard for the Centre College football team the previous year, and Dick played tackle next to me. Dick would say that I played guard next to him, but that would be incorrect; Dick played tackle next to me. I want that point to be perfectly clear in case he ever reads this book! Anyway, when I was a senior, I was laying on the ground stretching when Dick walked up and told me I should apply for a job with IBM in Lexington, KY. I had never heard of IBM, but Dick said they paid well, so I said, sure, I'll apply. I got the job and was awarded the coveted title of "junior programmer."

My early career was spent in a single location moving up the ranks and learning everything I could possibly absorb. I spent the last 20 years of my IBM career working in customer locations and interacting with executive management on a daily basis. I am very fortunate to have had the opportunity to learn from my customers, many of whom I count among my very best friends today. It was during these years that I formed my thoughts around the career management process I'm going to describe in this book.   In 2010, I joined Nationwide Insurance.   As the new guy with 30 years of outside experience, I was sought out by many people as a mentor. I was at Nationwide when my mentee and friend suggested I write a book about my process. So, here I am writing a book, for people interested in a career.

This is not a book for "job jumpers."   You know the type. Job jumpers are people who want to move up the ladder as fast as they possibly can. They apply for a new job, maybe even at another company, as soon as they start a job. They don't care if they're qualified for a job. They just want to keep moving up the ladder.   Job jumpers don't have careers; they have jobs.   They rise to and sometimes beyond their level of competence. Job jumpers, this book is not for you. It's for people who are interested in a career, not just the next job. It's for people who want to stay in a job long enough to learn as much as possible so they can perform better and learn more in the next job. This book is for people who want to become more valuable to an employer and have the opportunity to be rewarded for their value through career advancement.

This isn't going to be like any other book you've read. I'm going to give you straight talk about how management views employees and how managers think when filling positions.   Everything I tell you is based on my interactions and experiences with the companies with and for whom I've worked. This is not a "feel-good" book. I'm not going to sugarcoat it for you. I'm going to tell it like it is from the first page to the last. I'm going to give you:

- advice based on real life the way it is in the corporate world
- the tools you'll need to take a hard look at yourself and your career
- a process to:
  - lay out a career plan and the tools to leverage that plan to the fullest
  - be more prepared to compete for a job
  - help you improve your chances of winning
  - help you feel more in control of your career

Throughout this book I will write as if I'm speaking to you sitting across the desk from me in my office. When you read "I", you should think "prospective employer."

Reading about Career Management can be a boring topic. I kept the chapters pretty short so you can read a chapter and take a break, or most likely a nap. I think short chapters also help to simplify the key points I'm trying to make.

You will also notice my occasional attempt at humor. While I use humor to make this book easier and more fun to read, I want to be perfectly clear – **your career is a very serious topic**. You need to be engaged and actively managing your career. This book will help you do that. Please enjoy the humor but don't let it distract from the seriousness of the topic.

The first thing I'm going to do is explain how to write a resume that will help you compete and win the jobs you want and need. Next, I'm going to show you how to construct your Career Plan — not just a plan to win your next job — but a plan that maps out potential next jobs that support your long-term career goals. And finally, I'll show you how to create a Network Plan aimed at building and maintaining key relationships.

When you finish this book, if you do what I suggest, you will know how to market yourself the RIGHT Way, at the RIGHT Time, to the RIGHT People!

Section 1: Resume Writing

The Resume

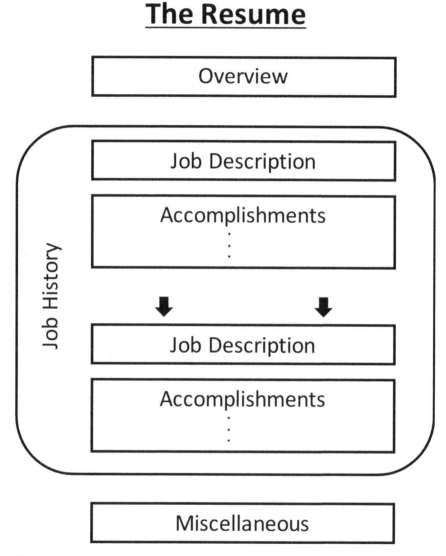

FIGURE 1: COMPONENTS OF A RESUME

Chapter 1: The Purpose of a Resume

Everybody has a resume, from graduating college seniors to professionals who have been in the workforce for years. A well-written resume is an essential tool when looking for a job. It's a device to showcase your experience to a prospective employer. It's a way to highlight the battles you've fought and won, and what you've learned along the way. It should demonstrate how successful you've been throughout your career.

Yes, all of the above is true to a degree. But I believe a resume has one and only one purpose, and that is to get an in-person interview. You might have a perfectly written resume on expensive, peach-colored, cotton paper, outlining your career in prose that an award-winning journalist would be proud of. But if it doesn't get you that interview, it is <u>worthless</u>. So how do you go about creating a resume that results in an interview? You're in luck! That's what this section is all about.

Before we get started, let me tell you some things that are absolute truths when it comes to creating a resume.

Truth #1: Make sure your resume is grammatically correct: free of spelling errors, punctuation errors, formatting errors and other mistakes that reek of

carelessness. Seems obvious, doesn't it? Well, I've read many resumes submitted for executive positions that were full of embarrassing mistakes. Your resume is the first indication I get as a prospective employer about your character and attention to detail. It's a reflection of how seriously you take things, and how much attention you will pay to detail when you are working for me. If you don't even take the time to spell check your own resume, what do you think that tells me about the quality of work you're likely to do for me? I can tell you what it tells me.... that I should throw your resume in the trash. When I run across the first mistake, I throw it away, because **there is no excuse for errors in a resume**. Proofread the resume. Have someone else proof it for you. And then do it again with someone else. Tell your proofreaders to <u>read s-l-o-w-l-y and read it solely for spelling and grammar</u>, not for content. I can't stress this point enough. It is the single most important tip I will give you in this chapter. And by the way, if English isn't your first language, that's no excuse to have grammar and spelling errors in your resume. If you need help, go get it!

Truth #2: It doesn't matter what your college GPA was unless you are applying for your first job right out of college. If you have five or more years of experience, that's what I want to hear about. I want to know what you've accomplished in your career so far because that might be exactly what I need. So please, don't give me your GPA once you have a reasonable amount of work experience. It isn't relevant anymore.

Truth #3: If your career spans 20+ years you only need to tell me about the last 15 years. Anything older than that is too old to influence my thinking. There are, however, two exceptions. First, if your resume shows me the last 15 years in detail, and then you give me a few sentences consolidating your previous employment as "various positions of increasing responsibility," I can live with that. Everyone starts their career as a *new employee* with specific responsibilities. I could argue that this was the best time of my working career. I worked my eight hours and then went to the pool at my apartment complex for the rest of the evening! I didn't know enough to have to take work home. But as those early years went by and I learned and progressed up the lower ladder rungs, I had some important learning opportunities. So don't blow off those years, describe them in a few sentences that represent your growth and learning.

The second exception is very important. If you have an experience or a skill set that is unique and hard to acquire, you need to say so in your resume. For example, if you ran your own business, that tells me that you have skills most lifetime corporate employees do not have. You've dealt with profit and loss pressures, people management, sales, etc. You have skills other people don't have!   Remember, I said a resume is supposed to get you an in-person interview.   Differentiating yourself with unique, hard-to-acquire skills is a way to persuade a hiring manager to bring you in for an interview.   Even if this experience is more than 20 years old, use it!

Now let's get back to the truths.   As a hiring manager, I don't want to read about how great you are at the job you already have.   Don't pigeon-hole yourself into the job you already have by telling me how great you are at it.   I want to understand how the skills and experiences you've acquired throughout your career can be applied to my needs.

Truth #4:   Write your resume to showcase your skills and how great you will be at the job that <u>I have</u> <u>that you want</u>.   Show me why I have to have you on my team!   You might be thinking this implies that you need to have multiple versions of your resume, one for each type of position for which you apply.   AHA!!!   You are correct!   If you were thinking you could write one great resume, put your feet up and wait for the calls to come in, well, you were simply mistaken.   Your resume has to be targeted to the position for which you are applying.   Let me read about how <u>your skills</u> apply to <u>my needs</u>. Make me want to talk to you.   That's the secret to resume writing.   How do you make me want to talk to you? We'll talk about that later in the following chapters.

Truth #5: Resume writing is hard. It takes work — hard work — and lots of it. You will write your resume, rewrite it, and rewrite it again many times. You will need friends to proofread your resume and give you feedback, sometimes brutal feedback, about how it reads and how you showcase yourself. My advice to you is to take all feedback in the spirit in which it was intended. Don't get defensive. Take the feedback, compile it with other feedback, and develop your own conclusions. Remember that feedback is just one person's opinion. You don't have to use it. You should however, seek out as much feedback as you can and use it to make your resume better.

I hope I haven't scared you off. If you've made it this far, you'll probably read the whole book. Good for you! That's the kind of tenacity I'm looking for as an employer. Now let's take a look at the components of a resume and discuss each one in detail.

Chapter 2: Resume Formats

Before we dive into the specific components of a resume, let's discuss resume formats. I've seen two basic resume formats: chronological and skill-based. In my opinion, chronological is the best fit for businesspeople. As an employer, I want to know as much as possible about a potential employee. With a chronological resume, I can analyze a person's career from their initial job through their current job. I gain insight into the path taken and the kind of work preferred. I can tell if a person is a "job jumper" or someone who wants to learn and grow as a valued member of a team. I can see the growth a person has experienced by the increasing responsibility each job required.

A skill-based resume is meant to depict specific abilities. It shows a person's primary area of expertise along with multiple other skills. The skill-based resume isn't meant to chronicle a person's career but rather to showcase a person's specific skills. I can see where this type of resume would be useful for an artist or actor but in the business world? Not so much. While I care about a person's current skill set, I also want insight into that person's growth, ability to learn and desire to progress in their career. The skill-based resume lacks all of these data points. Remember that I usually have at least 10 to 15 resumes from which to choose the select few who will get an in-person interview. Getting that interview is the main purpose of a resume, isn't it? You don't want me to have any doubts about your background and abilities! That's why I recommend using a chronological resume. It's the best tool for the job.

Now let's get on with the Job History…

Chapter 3: Job History

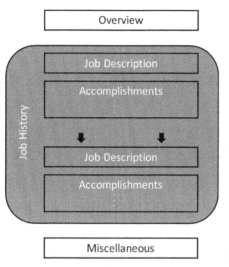

The objective of this section is to show me how you've grown throughout your career. Your description of each job should provide insight into the breadth and depth of the work to which you've been exposed. Your Job History should start with the most recent job and progress through earlier jobs. As I read your resume from your earliest job to your current job, I should be able to see the ever-increasing job responsibilities you've tackled. I should see growth via promotions and job opportunities given to you by previous managers. These tell me they believed in your potential and took the time to invest in you! When you finish the description of each job in your resume, read it from the back page to the front. I promise you that I will. See how your career reads to you. Read it from my perspective as the hiring manager and make the necessary adjustments to ensure your career shows your skill and experience growth and your desire to continue to progress and learn.

Now let's discuss what each individual Job Description should include. The purpose of a Job Description is to

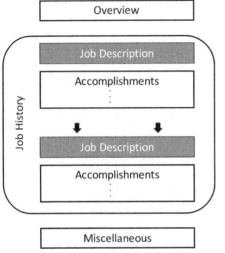

showcase the breadth and depth of the job. It's your chance to show how important the job was to your employer and the various skills required to perform in the position. **This is where you document the job responsibilities, not in the Accomplishments section!** We'll talk about accomplishments later. This section is all about the job and is your chance to tell me that you were entrusted with a lot of responsibility in this particular role. This is not a one-sentence description. It will take three or even four sentences to explain the points you need to get across.

Warning! Do not use this section to tell me about the company for which you worked. I can't tell you how many times I've received a resume from someone who worked for a Fortune 100 company and chose to waste precious resume space to tell me about AT&T or IBM. I guess they thought it would impress me to know how many people AT&T employed and how much global revenue IBM earned. Trust me, it doesn't. I want to know about you and the job you held at AT&T or IBM. Don't waste your chance to impress me with useless facts.

Let's talk about the few key areas to get into a Job Description that will impress me:

1. **Job title, dates in job, location:** Obviously I need to know this information. The only point I want to make here is to be sure to use a job title that is recognized by the industry. You want to be sure I understand the job as much as possible from the job title. For example, when I ran outsourced accounts at IBM my job title was "Project Executive". The title was known within IBM and conveyed the experience and skills required for the job. But outside of IBM it wasn't recognized. So, if you were to read my resume you would see a job title of "Account Executive," the industry job title that most closely aligned to my role.

2. **Management:** If you were responsible for managing a team of people, say so. I will want to know you have people management experience.

3. **Size - people or $:** Tell me about the magnitude of the job. Did you manage or lead 10 people or was it 75? Can you add something about the amount of money you were entrusted to manage? Let me be clear: I don't care that you supported the sales department that had annual revenue of $500 million.

I want to know specifically what <u>you</u> were accountable to manage. For example, if you managed a team of application developers that created a piece of software that enabled the sales team to realize $500M of sales, tell me about the work to create the software. However, if you actually did manage the sales program that resulted in $500M of sales, cool, tell me that!

4. **Profit and loss:** Were you responsible for managing within a "cost-only" budget or did you have responsibility for cost, revenue generation and profit attainment?

5. **Location / type of resource:** This is a key area that most people neglect to include in their Job Description. Managing people that sit next to you is a skill, for sure. Managing people that are geographically removed from you is an additional skill. And if the teams are in a different country, well, now you're telling me this job required management of a culturally diverse labor force! The type of resource managed is also important. If this job required management of a team of employees, vendors and customers, you're telling me the job required building a team of diverse resources, some of which weren't under your direct management control. All of these give you a competitive advantage and should be included in your Job Description.

6. **Level of interaction:** All jobs require interaction with other people. Did this job require interaction at the Director level? Vice President? Or did the job require regular interaction with C-level executives? Can you see why it's important to include this in the Job Description? The higher the level of interaction, the larger the scope of responsibility and the more political maturity required to succeed; that's the information you need to communicate.

Let's take a look at a few examples and dissect their content.

EXAMPLE 1
Job title: Director, Application Development

I managed a team of people to develop a new application to support Company ABC's rollout of a new inventory tracking system which saved over $500 million annually.

EXAMPLE 2
Job title: Director, Application Development

Responsible for management of a 60+ person team of geographically dispersed, global resources, including contractor and associate resources. Managed $50 million, three-year project through all phases of the application development life cycle including inception, requirements, software development, test, implementation and global rollout. Provided regular, direct communication to customer CEO and regional CIOs.

Which example do you prefer, 1 or 2? Example 1 tries to use one sentence to show how much the business depended on completion of the project. Hey, $500 million annual savings is great. But it doesn't tell me anything about the job. Conversely, there is a wealth of information, direct and implied, in Example 2. For example, I can tell that this person was responsible for:

- Managing people
- Leading a team greater than 60 people
- Managing people in other locations, maybe 10 miles away, maybe 6,000 miles away. This job required a good process to manage remote resources (I'll have to ask more in the interview).
- Managing resources in another country and culture which has a specific set of challenges that need to be thoroughly thought out.
- Managing resources not under their direct control. This requires good relationship building, especially with management of the customer resources involved.
- Controlling a $50 million budget over a three-year period. This tells me that this is "cost-only"

financial management, with budgeting requirements for future time periods.

- Leading the project from start to finish and having complete knowledge of the application development life cycle.
- Planning and executing the global rollout which tells me that this person had to manage rollout issues with vendors in other countries through other people.
- Developing direct relationships with C-level executives in the customer shop. And even though the resume didn't specifically say C-level interaction in the ABC Company and contracting companies, it is obviously part of the job.

Hopefully this example showed how you can put a lot of information into just a few sentences. Now that you know how to describe the job, it's time to explain how well you performed in the job. Let's move on to the next section of the resume, "Accomplishments".

Chapter 4: Accomplishments

Okay, so now I know the breadth and depth of each position you've held. That's great! But I still want to know what your achievements were in the job. Did you simply take up space for a few years? Did you perform the duties of the job without stretching yourself to deliver more than the average person would have delivered? Or did you execute the job responsibilities, look for ways to make things better, and improve things while you were there? Get what I'm talking about?

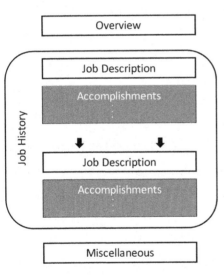

The Accomplishments section is your chance to tell me what you got done in the job. It's your chance to show that you aren't an average performer, just going through the motions. It's your opportunity to show that you improved your skills, acquired new experiences, and learned and grew while helping the organization realize significant accomplishments.... accomplishments that I need too!

Some people think writing about your accomplishments in a resume is "blowing your own horn." Well, in a way I guess it is. But the purpose of a resume is to get an interview. You can't get an interview with me unless I want to talk to you about your capabilities and accomplishments. But trust me on this: I will not want to talk to you unless you show me what you've accomplished in your career, and that you are capable of doing the same thing for me. You need to blow your horn!

Let's look at this from another perspective. How would you market a fantastic product? You would advertise all the great things the product can do. You would talk about why your product is the best one for the job. Well guess what? **YOU are the only product.** **YOU** are the only product you have to market, so why wouldn't you talk about all the great things you can do and have already done? And why wouldn't you talk about why **YOU** are the best product for the job? The answer is, you should! Now don't get me wrong — no one likes a braggart. But there is a difference between boastful arrogance and simply stating the facts about your career. Be honest, straightforward and factual in your documentation and you'll be fine.

So, what is an accomplishment? How do you go about writing one? I will admit there is an art to it, and it will take time. In fact, a lot of people simply can't get the right words out of their head and onto a piece of paper to write an impactful accomplishment. Heck, some people can't even remember what they accomplished 10 years ago! So what do you do if you find your brain in vapor lock? You do a brain dump! Write everything you can remember about each job you've had, including what was done, how it was done, results you remember, etc. I don't care if it's a full page or even two or three pages, just get it all down on paper. Walk away for a few days to allow your brain to reset itself. Then pick one of the jobs and read the data. Combine and reword your thoughts into cohesive, impactful statements. Walk away again and repeat. After a few iterations you should have several strong accomplishments.

So what is a "strong" accomplishment and how do you write one? I've seen accomplishments written well and I've seen them written very poorly. In my opinion, an accomplishment should be written as an action statement. You're telling me what you did to create an outcome or fix a problem. Use action verbs to relay that sense of energy. Next, every accomplishment should have the same basic components to ensure the hiring manager understands the situation and why you believe what you've written is a career accomplishment. A strong, impactful accomplishment statement has to contain: 1) the problem or situation you faced, 2) the action taken, and 3) the result of your action. If any component is missing, the accomplishment will look incomplete and your message will lose the impact you desire.   Keep in mind that the accomplishment doesn't have to be written in that order: problem, action, result.   Each accomplishment should be worded and organized to have the most impact on the reader.   For   example,   which   of   the   following accomplishments has the most impact?

Situation: You were the leader of a team that included technicians and businesspeople.   Your mission was to reduce severity 1 defects, currently averaging over 40 per month, to as few as possible as quickly as you could.   You were able to get under 10 defects per month in roughly eight weeks.

Option 1:

Participated on a team brought together to analyze defects and reduce severity 1 defects to fewer than 10 per month.

Option 2:

Reduced severity 1 defects by 75%+ in two months through aggressive leadership of a team of technical and business experts.

I'd say Option 2, wouldn't you?   First, the result is far more impactful as the lead-in for the accomplishment statement.   It hits the reader right in the eye: "Reduced severity 1 defects by 75%+..."   Second, doesn't "75%+" sound much stronger than "fewer than 10", especially when the reader isn't aware of the starting point of more than 40 defects?   Third, if you are the leader of the team don't be afraid to say so.   Remember, **YOU** are the only product you have to market.   Take credit for the things you've done in your career.   Fourth, the action taken is "aggressive leadership" of a team consisting of both technical and business areas.   This piece of information is very important and tells me that you have the skill to take different groups of people with varying interests, mold them into a team, and achieve the desired result.   Why would anyone leave this piece of information out?   And finally, stating the timeframe as "two months" rather than "eight weeks" makes it sound like a shorter period of time. I know it's the same, but subconsciously the reader is going to see "two" instead of "eight."

Now that we know how to write an accomplishment, how many do we need?   Most consultants lean towards three to six accomplishments for each job.   If you spent any amount of time in a job, you should be able to come up with three accomplishments.   If you have more than six, you should consolidate your accomplishments into fewer, more powerful statements.   It is important to note that an accomplishment doesn't have to be a single sentence.   It can be two or even three sentences.   The point is to use concise, pinpointed statements to create accomplishments that make the reader want to know more about how you did it.

One final word about accomplishments: use a thesaurus. Trust me on this, just buy one or find one online and please use it. I've received many resumes over the years that have line after line starting with "Managed." It's dull, it lacks imagination, and it leaves the reader unenthused about the content. In the previous chapter on page 20, I used a form of "managing" four times in five bullet points. Did you notice? Pretty dull wasn't it? I should have used supervised, led, oversaw, etc., to spice it up a bit.

What do you do with all the miscellaneous information that helps me understand more about who you are as a human being? Let's go to the next chapter and find out!

Chapter 5: Miscellaneous Information

At the bottom of the last page of the resume is the section we reserve for all those miscellaneous items. This is the place to put all the important information about you that isn't related to your work history. Miscellaneous items include but are not limited to:

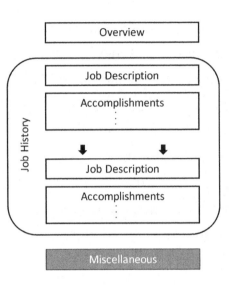

- Education History
- Professional Affiliations
- Personal Interests

Your education history is arguably the most important piece of information in this section and in your resume with the exception of your work history. Here is where you tell a prospective employer where you went to college, when you graduated and what degree(s) you earned. I've already said this once but let me say it again: unless you are a recent college graduate I don't care about your GPA. Think about it — for most people college is the first opportunity to be totally independent from Mom and Dad.

A successful college career, i.e., great GPA, tells me that you have the ability and discipline to accomplish things on your own without your parents harping at you every minute of the day. This is an extremely important piece of information for a recent college graduate. However, your GPA becomes less important every year. After five years of employment I'm more interested in your accomplishments in a work environment. Were you able to translate that college success into the work environment? What kind of work ethic have you displayed? Did you integrate well into the culture and team effectively with others?

The next most important piece of information in the Miscellaneous section is a list of your Professional Affiliations. As an employer I am interested in the level of commitment you have to your profession and career. If you are a project manager and you belong to the local chapter of the Project Management Institute, that tells me you are always trying to learn and grow your skills. List all of your professional affiliations, not just the important ones. But keep it to just the professional ones. You can add your personal items in the Personal Interests section.

In the Personal Interests section, you can add anything that tells me something about you. For example, you should tell me if you are active in a local charity, coach little league teams, play sports in the community, paint, love to read, etc.   Don't write a novel here, but tell the few things that are most important to you in your life. Remember, you're trying to tell me about you as a person. As an employer, I am interested in people who are invested in the community.   It gives me reassurance that you live here and take an interest in making our community a better place to live.   Definitely tell me if you hold a leadership position.   It is a great way to show your desire and ability to lead.

That's it for the resume...   not quite actually.   Now on to the most important part! Let's move to the next chapter and talk about the Overview.

Chapter 6: Overview

We've worked our way through the resume from front to back. Now we're going all the way back to the beginning, at the top of the first page. I know, I know. How could I have forgotten the first section of the resume? I didn't. **The Overview section is the most important part of your resume but it is the**

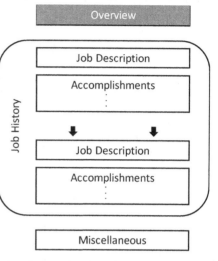

last section you will write! It is the culmination of all the hard work you put into writing the rest of your resume. It is the conclusion of the story of your work life. And it's the first thing you want me to read, right up front. So why would the conclusion of your life's work be the first part of a resume?

Unless you are seeking a position at the very highest levels, it is likely that I will receive a dozen or more resumes after filtering from the HR department. I have an open position so I'm pretty busy because I get to do the work until someone is hired. If I'm pressed for time it is unlikely that I will read every page of every resume brought forward. Even if I read every one, I will pay attention to the detail of only a select few. The Overview is how you make your resume one of those select few! The Overview is what makes me realize I need to read the rest of your resume. A good Overview shouts, "Don't you dare put me down! You need me on your team. Read on to learn more about me!"

I'm not going to lie to you — the Overview is the hardest part of your resume to compose. But if done right it is the most powerful paragraph you will ever write! It basically has two sections: the narrative overview and a bulleted list of significant skills. The narrative is comprised of a set of phrases describing a fundamental message about you or your career that points directly to something you documented in your work history. For example, if your Overview states "experience in multiple industries and geographies...," I should be able to see experience in multiple industries and geographies documented in your work history and/or Accomplishments.

The narrative Overview is not a long section. It should consist of three to five well-constructed sentences that paint a broad summary of your career and you as a person. Combining the appropriate phrases into powerful, meaningful statements is an art. I struggled with it and required professional help for my own resume — I simply couldn't get the phrasing just right. So don't be afraid to ask for help to critique and write your Overview.

The list of key skills is very simple. It is a list of skills you possess that are critically important to do well in the job for which you are applying. The list should be four to eight items at the most. Don't write sentences, just put the skills down on paper. For example, don't write "highly skilled in managing projects in all phases of development through implementation...." This isn't the place for a dissertation. Just state "project management." You just want me to get the point that you are a project manager. I will get additional detail in the Job History section of your resume.

Let's take a minute to dissect a well-written Overview.

INFORMATION TECHNOLOGY EXECUTIVE

Innovative, self-motivated leader with global perspective and experience in all aspects of information technology within large multi-national corporations across diverse industries. Uses excellent communication skills to forge partnerships with all levels of management. Applies a straightforward, hands-on style to skillfully resolve conflicts, build consensus, and motivate teams towards common goals.

Contract Management • Operations • Conflict Resolution

Notice that this Overview doesn't use a sentence to describe every statement. Every few words tells me something. Just the first sentence tells me this person won't require daily guidance. The person has global experience in very large corporations revealing political savvy, and the experience spans different cultures that exist in different industries. The second sentence reveals probable C-suite experience, verbal and written communication skills, and the desire and ability to develop relationships to get things done. The last sentence tells me the person is very direct and isn't afraid to dig into the detail. She has leadership ability and can bring a diverse set of people together to solve problems. Finally, it very directly states she is an expert in contract management, operations and conflict resolution. Do you see how much they told us? And she only used a little bit of resume space to do it!

Now before you get too giddy, remember that the assertions in the Overview must be proven with detail in the Job History section. If I don't see the proof in the Job History I have to assume it isn't true. That's why I recommend writing the Overview after you've written the rest of your resume. It's easier to pick out the things you want to emphasize from a written document than it is to try to write details to prove your Overview!

That's all there is to writing a resume, folks. It sounds straightforward and easy to do, but in reality it is very difficult. The beauty of it is that once you complete your resume, you never have to write it again!... NOT!!!   As you progress in your career, you will need to add new items to your Job History, education, etc., and you will want to enhance your Overview with new, powerful information.   So yeah, you don't have to rewrite your resume per se, but you will need to keep it current, make the occasional tweak to improve it or tailor it to a particular job.

Section 2: Building a Career Plan

The Career Planning Process

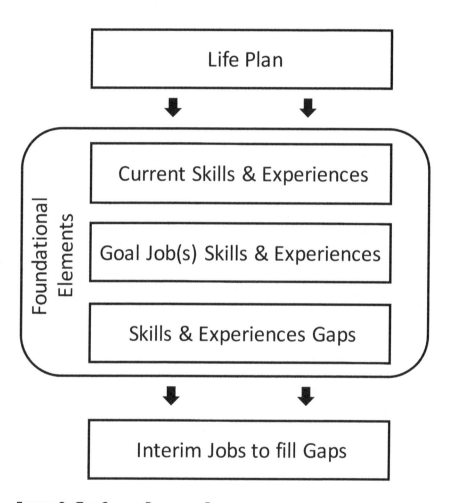

FIGURE 2: THE CAREER PLANNING PROCESS

Chapter 7: Introduction to Career Planning

In this chapter, we're going to switch gears completely. We're going to talk about how you go about creating a Career Plan and how you use that plan to manage your career. "Career" is the key word. As I said, this book isn't for "job jumpers." It's for people who want to improve themselves through skill development and experience, systematically improving their worth to the company and consequently rising up through the ranks and into the executive levels. A career doesn't happen in a year or even a decade. It's a lifelong endeavor spanning 30, 40, or sometimes even 50 years!

Fifty years! Whew, that's a little overwhelming, eh? Yup it is, and that's why you don't try to manage a 50-year career as a single entity; you break it up into smaller time periods. What is the right time period, you ask? I believe the right horizon is about 5 to 10 years for several reasons. First, we're talking about a career here, not the next job that seems cool and interesting. If I had a dollar for every time someone came to talk to me about their career and all they really wanted was advice on what to do next.... well, I wouldn't be a millionaire but I'd have a lot more money in my bank account!

The second reason I believe 5 to 10 years is the right timeframe is because five years is the minimum amount of time necessary to make <u>at least two</u> career moves. Likewise, the third reason is that no one can predict what life will be like in 10 years, much less beyond. A 10-year plan provides enough time to make a few moves, alter the plan if necessary, and still reach your goal. Why 5 to 10 years rather than just 5 or 10 specifically?   Different people have different goals with different opportunities and risks, different starting points, different ideas about the velocity of change they can handle, different life circumstances, and more. Hopefully you agree with me or are at least convinced that 5 to 10 years is a good timeframe.   If not, and 8 to 12 makes you feel better, go for it.   The point is to use a timeframe that is long enough to make multiple positive steps forward but not so long that you can't see the end of the tunnel.

So what's the first step?   Before we get into that I want to make an obvious statement, but one that requires discussion.   I want you to remember that your *work* life is part of your *real* life.   And *real* life changes... a lot! Marriage, divorce, children, aging parents; the list goes on. The point is, as life goes, so goes your career plan.   Life changes will cause you to change your plan.   Your plan should be focused on a realistic goal that can be reached within 5 to 10 years.   But you should be willing to change your plan to support life changes and, more importantly, the life you want to live.   The vast majority of the people I know work to support the life they want to live.   If you are one of those few people who live to work, you can skip the next chapter.   You won't care what I'm going to say, but if you are in the majority, read on!

Chapter 8: The Life Plan

Step 1: Don't create the Career Plan... Yet

The first step in the creation of the Career Plan is to hold off on creating that Career Plan. Yeah, you read that right. I said hold off on creating the plan... until you understand what you want your life to be like in the next 5 to 10 years. Think about it — since you're reading this

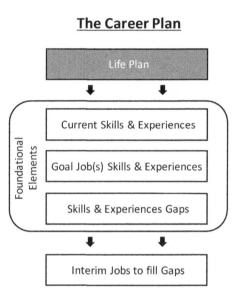

The Career Plan

paragraph I know you work to support the life you want to live. So why would you start planning your career before you figure out your life plan?   I'm not talking about making monumental decisions about your life. Don't put that much pressure on yourself.   But I am saying you should think about your life and ensure you understand what you want out of your life. One thing you probably already know is that you will pay a price for every step you take up the corporate ladder. You need to be sure the price you will pay is an acceptable impact to your life plan. For example, if you're a single person, do you intend to be single 5 to 10 years from now?   That might mean that travel or moves are an acceptable price to pay. It might also mean that you have to put your social life on hold for several years. If you have a new family with very young children, a move might mean leaving parents who are your primary source of babysitting. If you're in your late 40s, a move to a new city might mean leaving aging parents who will need your help over your current Career Plan timeframe. What if your kids are just getting old enough to play sports? Do you want to be able to coach their teams? Do you want to be home to see every game? Every practice? Is the next step up the ladder important enough to you to miss putting your kids to bed at night and being part of the bedtime story ritual? If you have to put in significant travel, is it an acceptable price to miss part of your spouse's and kids' lives? These are the things that you need to think about before creating your Career Plan.

The point is that whether you are married or single, you need to sit down and have at least one serious conversation about what you want your life to be like over your current planning horizon. At this point, don't worry about your Career Plan. We'll come back to that later. Just focus on thinking through your life and figuring out what you want your life to be like over the next 5 to 10 years.

Step 2: What Floats Your Boat?

Now that you have an idea of what you want your life to be like, let's talk about the second step in the development of your Career Plan. Where do you want to be in your career in the next 5 to 10 years? Don't think about every step along the way; we'll get to that in a bit. Just think about where you want to be when this planning timeframe is done. Do you expect to have experienced a promotion? Perhaps two? Or do you expect to acquire new skills and experiences in preparation for future opportunities?

You might be asking yourself, "How do I figure out what I want at the end of the planning timeframe?" Good question! Over the years, I've seen people go through this exercise in a number of ways. Some people are motivated by level and title. They tend to define success over a timeframe by achieving new levels in the organization. Others aren't interested in the title itself, but are motivated by the salary and benefits associated with a title. And others determine where they want to be by listing the things they love to do every day, and then listing the jobs that will allow them to enjoy those activities. My advice is to think about what motivates you and makes you want to get out of bed in the morning. Figure out what jobs will allow you to do the things you most enjoy and use one or two of these as the goal for your planning timeframe.

Step 3: Get Aligned

Okay, now you know what you want your life to be like and where you want your career to be in the next 5 to 10 years. Kudos to you! Now for the million-dollar question: Do they match? If you reach your career goal, will you be able to live the life you want to live along the way? If the answer is yes, HOORAY! You are ready to commit yourself to your career plan without worrying about the impact to your life or your family. Most people feel a sense of calm and relief when their career and life plans are mutually supportive of one another. But what if your answer was no, your Career Plan doesn't allow you to live the life you want to live? Now what? The solution is simple. Sit down with your spouse (or yourself if you're single) and discuss the implications of your Career Plan to your life plan. These conversations can be difficult, but they are necessary. It's better to make career or life decisions up front in full agreement with your spouse than to put yourself into a position where you don't have as many options. At this point, you may decide to alter your goal for this time period or determine that the potential impact to your life is acceptable based <u>on your situation at this time in your life</u>. That's okay! Remember, life changes. You might reverse your decision in a year or two or three. All you can do right now is make your decisions based on the information you have at your disposal at this moment in time. You will need to repeat this process until your life plan and your career plan are compatible with each other. Now, you're ready for the next step in the career planning process: assessing where you are in your career, what it takes to realize your goal and what gaps you need to close to get there.

Chapter 9: Skills & Experiences & Gaps, Oh My!

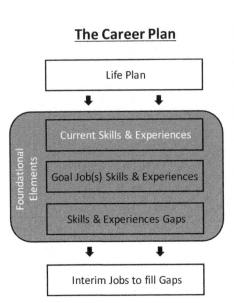

The Career Plan

Life Plan

Foundational Elements

Current Skills & Experiences

Goal Job(s) Skills & Experiences

Skills & Experiences Gaps

Interim Jobs to fill Gaps

Hiring managers are looking for people who have the skills and experiences to solve problems. With the exception of a new college graduate, I look for someone who can demonstrate the skills they possess and the experiences they've had that make them uniquely qualified for my position. So the next step in the career planning process is to assess your skills and experience. Before we start, let's discuss the difference between a skill and an experience.

SKILL,

noun:

1. The ability to do something well; expertise.
2. A particular ability.

EXPERIENCE,

noun: Practical contact with and observation of facts or events.

verb: Encounter or undergo (an event or occurrence).

Clearly skills and experiences are two different things. As the definition implies, a skill represents something about you; it's a particular expertise or ability that you possess. For example, you might know a particular programming language, or maybe you are a chemical engineer. Maybe you've been blessed with public speaking skills, or maybe you have in-depth financial management skills.

In simplest terms, an experience is the application or acquisition of a skill(s). It represents a situation in which you were able to use your skills and learn from the result (good or bad), as well as the journey you went through to realize the result. Let's say you have in-depth financial management skills. Have you undergone the experience of applying those skills in a small company, perhaps even as the Chief Financial Officer (CFO)? Have you worked in a large multinational firm applying your skills to international finance? Have you worked as a financial planner applying your skills in a different way? Get the point? Experiences tell me what you've been through in your career. They give me an idea of the environments in which you've worked, the kind of people with whom you've had to interface and much more. One last point on experiences — an experience can be a life lesson, completely unrelated to your working life. If you have a key life experience that improves your marketability, list it.

Hopefully you can see why both skills and experiences are important in career planning. At this point, all you have to do is think about yourself and write down all of your skills and experiences! Simple, right? Well, yes and no. There are two things to consider: 1) creating an accurate and honest list of your skills and experiences as perceived by you and others, and 2) representing the list in a way that is easy to understand and communicate.

What you need to do to create your list is sit down and start listing your skills and experiences, making sure to keep the two separate since they are very different. This will be useful when you leverage your lists with the people on your Network Plan (I'll explain this later). Be sure to assess yourself honestly. If you have a skill or experience, list it. If you don't, don't list it. This can be a tough conversation to have with yourself, but in my experience most people know themselves pretty well and can create an honest list of their skills and experiences.

Any easy way to document your lists is to draw a box and then draw a line vertically down the middle of the box.

Label the left side "Skills" and the right side "Experiences." List your skills and experiences in the appropriate column. Label this "Current" to represent where you are today. When you're finished you should have something like Figure 3: Skills & Experiences.

Current	
Skills	**Experiences**
Project mgt	Customer interaction
Systems engineering	Ran family business
Web design	Military

FIGURE 3: SKILLS & EXPERIENCES

Now that you have your list, how do you know it's accurate? Yup, honest does not equal accurate. What I mean is, your perception of your skills and experiences may not be consistent with what other people think about you. So how do you create a list that is not only honest but accurate? You guessed it: ask other people.

You may have noticed that I didn't talk about gaps in this chapter. Don't worry, we'll cover gaps in Chapter 13: Putting it All Together. In order to discuss how to define and deal with gaps we need to validate where we are, determine where we want to be, and determine the skills and experiences required to compete.

Chapter 10: Validating Where You Are

There are lots of ways to get other people's opinions. For example, you can simply ask a person what skills they think you possess. You can describe a situation you've encountered and the experience you believe you acquired. See if they agree with your assessment of yourself. Or you can ask your best friends what they think. After all, they know you really well, don't they? While both of these approaches will work, I believe the most effective method is to write it down and show your list to people, discuss why you believe the list is accurate and solicit their brutally honest opinions. Be sure they understand that your desire is to improve yourself, make yourself more marketable and progress through your career. Therefore, you want their honest assessment of your skills and experiences, even if it's something you don't want to hear.

How do you pick the <u>RIGHT People</u> with whom to discuss your lists? Begin by selecting people you respect and trust to give you an honest opinion. Look at people who are in a position to help you attain your goals for the current plan timeframe. Showing this group that you are serious about developing yourself, you have taken the time to organize your thoughts succinctly and you think enough of them to ask their opinion will help you create stronger relationships.   Remember, level isn't the only arbiter in selecting the <u>RIGHT People</u>.   People in positions lower than yours will provide insights that upper management cannot provide, so be sure to include people that will have differing views.   Be thoughtful about the people you choose to review your skills but don't fret about it.   The bottom line is that every conversation will provide insight, so there are no wrong decisions.

Chapter 11: Further Defining Where You Want to Be

Once you've determined where you are in your career, it's time to define in more detail, 1) where you want to be and 2) what you want to be like at the end of this 5 to 10-year timeframe. In Chapter 7: Introduction to Career Planning, we discussed aligning your personal life goals with your career goals.   It's time to create a Career Plan that puts more definition behind your career goals and outlines the path to achieve them.   First let's discuss how to determine where you want to be.   I'm a firm believer in the idea that a person has to understand what the answer needs to be before beginning to map out a path to get there. What I mean is, how do you know the step you're taking right now is on the correct path leading towards your goal? Let me say it another way — let's assume you live somewhere in the eastern United States.   Have you ever put your family on a plane heading for Europe and then called a family meeting on the plane to talk about where you want to go on vacation?   No, of course not!   What if you decide your destination is Hawaii?!   You've just wasted a lot of time and money taking a step in a direction that doesn't lead you where you want to go.   If you wouldn't go on vacation without a plan, why would you go on your career journey without one?   Why would you take that risk with your career?

Now that I've convinced you that you need to decide where you want to be at the end of the timeframe, the question becomes, how do you figure out where you want to be? The answer is to determine what motivates you and jot it down. Are you motivated by money? Title? Both? Or are you interested in money and title, but would rather have a job that allows you to do the things that excite you? Do you want to position yourself for a relocation? Think about what gets you out of bed in the morning. Think about your most satisfying moments in your life and career and determine what it was that created that satisfaction. Write it down in the left column of a chart like Figure 4: Likes & Dislikes.

What do I love to do	Take it or leave it	What do I hate to do
People interaction Problem solving Coaching other people Leading teams Project / Program Management	Status reporting Data analysis Database management	Presentations Public Speaking People Management

FIGURE 4: LIKES & DISLIKES

Conversely, think about the times you were in a living hell and write down what it was that made those situations so distasteful you want to avoid jobs with similar characteristics. Write that down in the right column. In the middle column write down the things that don't matter to you. Once you've finished this exercise, you should have a good list of the characteristics that make up your dream job! The next step is to identify jobs that have some of the characteristics on your list. I say "some" because it's unlikely that any job will have 100% of the things you would like to have. Create a list of jobs that have as many desirable characteristics as possible, but be careful to only list jobs that are realistic to obtain in your current time period. For example, if you've never been in management, you shouldn't include the CEO job on your list. It isn't likely you will rise from non-manager to CEO in a 10-year period. Once you have a list, pare it down to 1 to 3 jobs. If your list is too small, you run the risk of missing opportunities, but conversely, if the list is too big, you won't be able to create a manageable plan to get there.

At this point you know how to determine what your goal job(s) should be for the current 5 to 10-year timeframe, or to put it another way, you know how to figure out "where you want to be." So let's step back and answer the second part of the question: "What do you want to be like when you get there?" What I mean here is that when you reach your goal, you will have changed. You will have changed based on the path you took and the particular experiences acquired on that path. My old math teacher used to tell me the shortest distance between two points is a straight line, which is true in a purely mathematical sense. However, in career management the shortest path may not be the best path. Think about the people who currently hold one of your goal jobs. What value do they bring? How do they handle themselves with superiors? Peers? Their team? Do you believe they are effective in their job? Do people speak highly of them? Do people have confidence in them as a leader? Do you respect them? Why? The answers to these questions are important when you start to create your Career Plan. Think about how enjoyable it would be to be just like each of them. If you decide you would love to be just like a particular person, take the time to understand the path they took to get where they are. Every one of them will have taken a different approach and will have their own unique set of skills and experiences that made them who they are. Emulate those who are admired by you and others.

Another aspect of thinking through "what you want to be like" is that it creates a transition from your current / goal state to the steps required to create a Career Plan. As you examine how those whom you respect have achieved the position you want, you will begin to see patterns emerge. Again, emulate those patterns if it makes sense and appeals to you. If not, it's okay to create your own unique path!

Chapter 12: Goal Job Skills & Experiences

The Career Plan

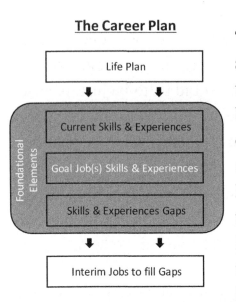

At the beginning of the "Career Plan" section, I said that a career can span up to 50 years and that the best way to manage a career is to break it up into shorter timeframes. What I didn't tell you is that all of these timeframes are tightly linked and that every timeframe relies on and builds on the results of the previous timeframes. In this context, you can understand that a more indirect route may better prepare you for greater opportunities and quicker advancement in future time periods. The point is that whether you emulate someone else's Career Plan or you create your own, you must be confident in your choices. You must have a self-assured point of view about why you are making the choices you are making. Remember that a Career Plan allows you to actively manage your career and put yourself in a position to compete for jobs. It does not guarantee that you will win every job you go after.

As you progress through your plan, remind yourself why you made the choices you made. When you have a setback, it's human nature to question everything you're doing.   Remind yourself why you created your Career Plan and why you made the choices you made. Too many people are looking for "the path" to success. They forget that it isn't just about getting to your goal, it's also about how you get there!

Now that you've defined your goal job(s), you need to build the list of skills and experiences required for each job exactly the same way you did in Chapter 9:   Skills &

Executive Level Program Mgr	
Skills	Experiences
Pgm mgt > $20M	Multiple programs
Project mgt	Sales systems
Exec communication	
Finance	
App Development	

FIGURE 5: GOAL JOB(S) SKILLS & EXPERIENCES

Experiences & Gaps, Oh My! If you aspire to be an Executive Level Program Manager your goal job might look something like Figure 5: Goal Job(s) Skills & Experiences. If you aren't familiar with what is required, how do you figure it out?   There are basically two ways. The first is to talk to your Human Resources department. Many companies have documented detailed descriptions of all roles within the company. These descriptions generally discuss the job requirements, breadth and depth of the job, and many other pertinent details people want to know. For our purposes, they represent the skills required to compete for the job. Job Descriptions also list a few mainstream experiences, such as "10 years of people management experience" or "experience managing off-shore resources." The second way to gather information about a job is to talk to people already in the job or people who interface with the people in the job. Showing interest in a job and talking to people familiar with it will get you the information you need, provide an opportunity to meet someone new who can help you with your career and subtly tell people about your desire to improve yourself and take on more responsibility to help the company. Trust me, every manager wants to know these kind of people!

Congratulations! At this point you now know <u>where you are</u> and <u>where you want to go</u>. All that's left to create your Career Plan is to determine the steps to get there. Let's go to the next chapter and see how that's done!

Chapter 13: Putting it All Together

In the next few chapters we're going to learn how to build a Career Plan. I'm going to explain how to use the information you compiled in the previous chapters to create multiple paths leading to your goal(s), and I'm going to explain how you can use your Career Plan to manage several situations you will undoubtedly experience in your career.

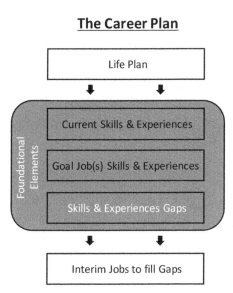

The Career Plan

Life Plan

Foundational Elements

Current Skills & Experiences

Goal Job(s) Skills & Experiences

Skills & Experiences Gaps

Interim Jobs to fill Gaps

You already created and verified two lists of skills and experiences.   The first, your current list, defined where you are in your career right now, and the second, your goal job list, defined where you want to be at the end of the current planning period.   It stands to reason that if you know where you are and where you want to be, you should be able to map out the steps to get there.   Think of it like an obstacle course.   You're standing at the starting line (you know where you are) but you can see the finish line (where you want to be).   You see and understand the obstacles in front of you, so you map out a plan to overcome the obstacles and realize your goal: the finish line. If you think about skill and experience "gaps" as the obstacles, the first step becomes obvious. You need to understand the obstacles in front of you so you can map out a plan (your Career Plan) to overcome them.

The first step to create a Career Plan is to compare your current skills and experiences to the skills and experiences required for the job(s) you want at the end of this planning period. The differences will become your third list and we'll call it your "gap list." Using the lists you created your gap list would look something like Figure 6: Gap List. The gap list isn't any more important than any other list you have, but it will become your planning period "bucket list," if you will. The gap list represents the skills and experiences you need to acquire to be able to realistically compete for the job(s) you want. Your gap list may be long if you're contemplating a career change or multiple promotions, or it may be short if you're working on rounding out your skill set for your current job family. It basically depends on where you are and where you want

GAPS	
Skills	**Experiences**
Pgm mgt > $20M	Multiple programs
Exec Comm.	Sales systems
Finance	
App Dev	

FIGURE 6: GAP LIST

to be. But the good news is that you'll have a clear list of things to work on to achieve your goals!

We have three lists. Let's put them together and see what they tell us. Step 1: take a piece of paper and place your current list in the lower middle part of the paper. Step 2: add your goal job to the top of the page. Step3: put your gap list in the lower left corner of the paper to the left of your current list. What you have in front of you is the foundation of your Career Plan for the current time period. It should look something like Figure 7: Career Plan Foundational Elements on page 62. It shows where you are now along with your current skills and experiences, where you want to be along with the skills and experiences required to compete for your goal job(s), and the skill and experience gaps you need to close to get there. Now it's time to create the plan to get there.

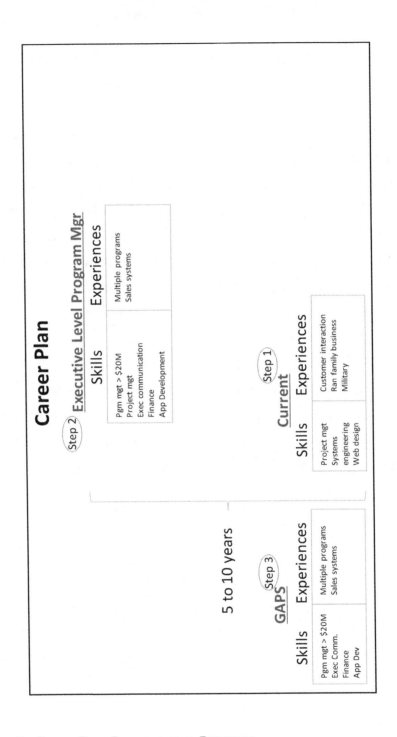

Figure 7: Career Plan Foundational Elements

Chapter 14: Building the Connections

As you look at your gap list, think about potential jobs that will move you towards your goals. Document the skills and experiences for each job just like you've already done for your current, goal job, and gap lists. Include jobs that interest you, jobs that you have noticed as potential stepping stones in your company, and jobs that close a skill or experience gap for you and create a list. Remember that it's okay to take a lateral move if it closes gaps! Be sure to note which skill and experience gaps are closed for each job. I want to note that taking on an extra assignment can result in a new skill or experience too! For the sake of clarity and easier reading, when I say "job" I'm talking about any activity that results in the acquisition of a skill or experience.

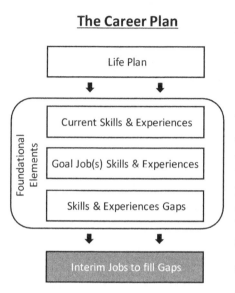

The Career Plan

- Life Plan
- Foundational Elements
  - Current Skills & Experiences
  - Goal Job(s) Skills & Experiences
  - Skills & Experiences Gaps
- Interim Jobs to fill Gaps

Before we continue, a word of warning — **guard against taking a job you've already done**. Do not take a job that affords little to no opportunity to grow in your career or personal space. Such a job is useless for your career. Be sure each job you have on your list represents a "stretch opportunity." What I mean is, every job you decide to take should make use of your current set of skills and experiences and it should provide the opportunity for you to acquire new skills and experiences that broaden your responsibilities and your thinking. Remember our resume conversation? I will read from the back page of your Job History to the front page to see if every step you've taken broadens your scope of responsibility and experience. I can't tell you the number of people that have come to me for career advice that have said, "I only take jobs I know how to do and have done before, so I can do them well and be successful." Essentially they are telling me they have a very limited skill set and don't have the confidence to take on new things. They're telling me they want to be comfortable in their job and never make a mistake. If that's true, my advice to these people is to give this book to someone else. But what I hope is that they simply haven't had good career coaching in previous years! In that case, my advice would be to read this book carefully and fully understand the messages herein. Plan a career that is challenging and exciting. Don't sit on the sidelines. Go for it!

Once you finish creating your job list along with the skills and experiences for each, begin to place the jobs on your piece of paper. Carrying our example forward, reference Figure 8: Sample Career Plan on page 68 as we walk through the next steps. Start with jobs that are logical next steps from your current job. Remember, your current set of skills should allow you to compete for these jobs right now. If the job is a lateral move, add it to the right of your current state. Add a job above your current state for a promotional move. Draw a line from your current state to each job to create a visual career path connection. Try not to have more than three or four connections or your plan will become unreadable and unmanageable. The point of this exercise is not to have the biggest map; it is to create a reasonable, clear and manageable map. Look at the jobs you just added to your paper. It is highly unlikely that each of these jobs satisfy the exact same set of gaps. If it makes sense to move between two jobs, draw a line to connect them. If it doesn't because there are minimal additional gap closures, other opportunities provide broader exposure, etc., then don't make the connection and consider removing this job from your plan.

The next step is to repeat the process starting with each job you just added to your paper. Continue to repeat until you can connect to your goal jobs. Once you can trace your way from your current state to your goal jobs, you are done.... almost. All you have to do now is to perform a quality check on your career roadmap. Look at the connections and be sure each path makes sense and moves you toward your goals. Add or remove connections as necessary.   If an area of your map looks too complex, it probably is and is likely not manageable.   In this case, rethink the jobs and connections and be sure they make sense.

If you find yourself thinking about getting a bigger piece of paper because you have so many potential jobs and so many connections that you simply can't clean it up, start over 'cause you've missed the point.   Use the KISS method: Keep It Simple, Stupid!   It simply isn't realistic to manage a plan that has 15 possible next steps for each job.   Decide on the paths that make sense for what you want to accomplish, keep it simple, and then manage your plan using your Network Plan which I'll talk about in the next chapter.

One other point — if you have more than three or four steps from your current job to your goal job(s), you should rethink your goal job(s).   In order to acquire new skills and experiences, I believe that you have to be in a job for two or more years.   Remember what I said in the introduction to this book: this process isn't for "job jumpers" or people chasing a title.   It's for people who want to proactively manage their career by smartly acquiring the right skills and experiences, becoming more valuable to the company, and moving along their chosen path to achieve their personal goals.

The last point I want to make about the Career Plan is to think about the connections between the jobs. Sometimes it only makes sense to move from job A to job B, but not vice-versa. If so, be sure to use an arrow denoting the direction in which your career should move. If you believe you need two particular jobs to close gaps and can take either job before the other, use a bi-directional arrow. The point is to use arrows to clarify the path and simplify your choices.

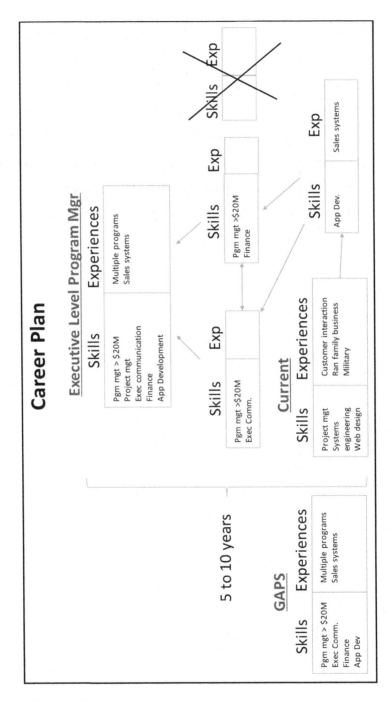

FIGURE 8: SAMPLE CAREER PLAN

Now it's time to sit back and admire your work. How do you feel? I hope you feel a little more in control of your own destiny. If you're still a bit apprehensive, not to worry! We still need to discuss the Network Plan, and how the Career Plan and the Network Plan complement each other. But before we go there, let's talk about a few career situations you may find yourself in and how the Career Plan will help you navigate through each one.

Chapter 15: Using the Career Plan

So you're sitting in a meeting with your mentor discussing your career like you've done many times before.   Chances are you're asking about jobs that just opened up.   Should you apply or not?   Do your skills qualify you?   What do people think about you, and are you a serious candidate for the job?   Your mentor answers your questions one by one and provides good advice, probably the same advice she provided the last time a job opened up that you thought you might enjoy. You get the same advice; you're frustrated.   She's giving the same advice and she's frustrated to talk about the same things again too! So what do you think would be different if you pulled out your Career Plan and — instead of talking about the job that just opened up — had a conversation about your career aspirations?   You show how you've thought through where you are and where you want to go.   You explain how you've thoughtfully determined where you are in terms of skills and experiences and what it will take to compete for your goal jobs.   You explain how you've researched jobs and built out the next few moves in your career.   And you sum up by asking what she thinks about your plan and if she has any advice for improvements. Then you wait….

In a few moments it will all register with her.   She will see that you are serious about your career.   She will see that you no longer need to discuss the job that just opened up.   Based on your Career Plan you already know if the job is something that can help you achieve your goals. Just by showing her your Career Plan, you've implanted several key subliminal messages.   First, you are serious about your career.   Second, you are well-organized and have the ability to create a long-term plan, complete with options.   Third, you respect and admire her as a mentor and as a colleague, hence the reason you are asking her opinion.   Fourth, you are playing to her ego (come on, all of us have an ego and we like to be asked for help).   She will be thrilled that you asked and will be personally invested in your success!   And that's exactly what you want in a mentor!

Turned out different than previous conversations, didn't it?   Rather than a mundane discussion about a job, you're having a real in-depth career conversation.   And you're letting her know that you are determined to reach your goals.   Keep in mind that this conversation isn't limited to your primary mentor.   It's a conversation you can have with all of your mentors (you should have more than one!). You can have this conversation with your current boss, former boss, even your future boss.   The point is you can use your Career Plan in many ways with lots of different people.   When combined with your Network Plan, you have a very powerful marketing toolkit with which to proactively manage your career!

THE "SHOTGUN" APPROACH

The "shotgun" approach to career planning is exactly what it sounds like. It's a random method of picking jobs across a wide spectrum of unrelated careers and job families. It's essentially like having no plan at all. The Career Plan you just created will help you avoid the many pitfalls of the shotgun approach. One of the worst is when a person gets labeled as a level chaser. You've seen this happen — someone wants to get promoted so badly he applies for every job at the level he desires, whether or not the job is within his career path, job family, or even his area of the company. Trust me, management is not stupid. It may seem like it at times. But truthfully, management is not stupid. If someone is applying for random jobs that all result in a promotion without any other forethought or planning, they will be labeled a level chaser. Once a person gets a label like that, it is nearly impossible to lose it. It will actually become a negative even when the person is really qualified for a job that would be a promotion.

Your Career Plan will show a finite list of potential jobs specifically for you. It will show management what each job will do for you and how it will prepare you for broader responsibility. By their absence, it will show that other jobs are of no interest to you because they don't move you towards your goals. You are not a level chaser and you don't take your career for granted. Your Career Plan creates a focused approach for your personal growth and your ever-expanding value to the company.

CHANGING THE PLAN

You have a 5 to 10-year plan. You've done a yeoman's job of marketing yourself by communicating your plan to others. Now that everyone has seen it you better not change it. Hogwash! Remember what I said previously in this book: Life happens. Things change. You can, and you should, revisit your Career Plan on an annual basis or when something changes in your career or in your life. For example, what if you take another job on your Career Path and you learn that you don't actually like what you're doing? Maybe you want to change your long-term goal job? That's okay. Your plan is not set in stone. Just go back to the beginning and work your way through the process again. It's really that simple.

TAKING A CAREER BREAK

Life happens — I can't stress that enough. What will you do if your parents become ill and you're faced with a decision to put them in a nursing home, move them in with your family, or even quit your job and move closer to your parents? No one really knows until the situation demands an answer. It's important to understand that you might have to put your career on hold for a while and take a break from moving up the corporate ladder. Please believe me when I tell you that it's okay. Everyone will go through a personal crisis at some point. It's called *life*. Do what you need to do for your family. When the situation changes, refresh your Career Plan and pick up where you left off.

YOU DIDN'T GET THE JOB – NOW WHAT?

We just talked about changing your Career Plan because you got a new job that was on the plan. What if you applied for a job on your plan and you didn't get it? What do you do? You learn from the experience. You should get feedback outlining why you didn't get the job. You might get feedback directly from the hiring manager or your own manager. Take the feedback with an open mind and analyze it. Don't be defensive. Don't be personally offended and refuse to listen to feedback. Remember, managers award jobs for lots of reasons. Sometimes the most qualified person doesn't get the job. So don't think it's about you as a person. Trust me, it usually isn't. But it might be next time if you don't respond appropriately... If the feedback seems thin, ask your mentor to request feedback. Sometimes the hiring manager will be reluctant to deliver a difficult message directly but will be more open and forthright with your mentor. You deserve to get feedback so you can improve. Expect it and do whatever it takes to get it.

Now that you've heard the feedback, you should discuss it and your Career Plan with your mentor, manager, and whomever else you trust. The feedback will provide valuable information about skills and experiences you lack, network connections you haven't managed appropriately (we'll discuss the Network Plan in the next chapter), or any number of other things. You might need to add another step in your plan, or perhaps change your Network Plan to address an issue. No matter what the feedback is, your Career Plan is a valuable tool in understanding how you are perceived and what changes are needed in your marketing plan. It's a tool to show that you want feedback so you can improve and bring more value to the table. And it shows management that you will not be deterred from your goal. You will listen, take action and move forward. And that's why you should get the next position you apply for!

HOW DO YOU KNOW WHEN YOU ARE READY FOR THE NEXT MOVE?

Probably the most frequently asked question I get is "how do I know when I'm ready for the next move?" I could write a lengthy chapter on this topic alone. When a person is thinking about changing careers or companies, the topic gets pretty broad. It's a great topic but unfortunately, it isn't the point of this book. So let me use the KISS method on this one. You know you are ready for your next move when you have acquired the skills and experiences you expected to acquire in the position you are currently in. Yup, it's that simple. Just ask yourself if you've accomplished what you expected to accomplish. Did you meet who you wanted to meet? Did you create the new network relationships your current job offered? Did you achieve the goals set forth by your boss when you took the job? Or more clearly, will your boss gladly help you get your next position because you did a great job and accomplished everything she needed and more? Or will she reluctantly let you go because you haven't finished the job yet? When you think about these questions the answer becomes pretty clear.

THE SO-CALLED "SPECIAL ASSIGNMENT" FROM THE BOSS

You've reviewed your Career Plan with your boss. She knows the potential next steps for you. But she comes to you and says she has a great opportunity for you; one that will really look good on your resume. If the opportunity fits into your plan, great! If it doesn't (Figure 8: Sample Career Plan on page 68 – note the big "x"), what do you do? Or maybe the boss asks you to take a job that she knows isn't on your plan (i.e. it doesn't provide any new skills or experiences) because she has a problem and you're the right person to fix it. Do you take the job or politely refuse? What if you don't have a choice, or in other words you can turn down the opportunity but it will reflect poorly on your willingness to help the company?

The answer to this problem is pretty simple: You take the job. First and foremost, you have to be willing to help the company out of a jam. If you aren't, then it will impact your ability to land the jobs you want. Management will question your loyalty and dedication to them and the company. But before you agree to the job, it is critical to review your Career Plan with your boss. Discuss the reason you built your plan in the first place: to map out the steps that will help you grow and become more valuable to the company. Point out that this job, while very important, doesn't help you grow as an employee and a person. You understand how important it is, and you are willing to help, but from a career perspective you are basically going on hold. Discuss how long your boss believes you will need to be in the job. Timeframes are usually negotiable to some degree. Have a discussion about the next job on your plan and ask your boss if she will help you get it after you help her out. It is a fair and reasonable discussion to have with your boss. If you are willing to make a sacrifice for the good of the company, then why can't the company help you with your career? Ninety-nine percent of the time your boss will gladly help you. I mean, think about it; she asked you to take this special opportunity because she knows you are capable of solving the problem for her. At the end of the day you have to be willing to take one for the team every now and then. But you should get something out of it too.

One more point before we move on. Discuss the possibility of getting additional exposure with senior management while you are on this "special assignment." For example, request an audience with your boss's boss to discuss the assignment and your next career move. There's no guarantee your boss will be around when you are ready for the next step. Make sure her boss is aware of your agreement and is willing to help as well. Ask who you will provide status to, and be sure you are the one who is front and center. Creating new network connections will be handy later in your career. Hey, as long as you're there you might as well make your "special assignment" as productive as possible for the future!

THE NETWORKING CONNECTION

We've discussed several ways to use your Career Plan to help manage your career and to manage your way through different situations. There's one more very powerful way to use your plan: to identify potential and necessary network connections. Think about it. You've mapped out every potential job you need to realize your goals in this time period.   You need to develop a relationship with every hiring manager for every job listed on your Career Plan.   If a hiring manager meets you for the first time in an interview, your chances of landing the job are way lower than if the manager already knows you and what you are capable of doing for him.

When you build your Career Plan for the first time, you can use it to populate your first Network Plan.   Going forward you will use each plan to complement the other. If something changes in your Career Plan, something may need to change in your Network Plan.   If something changes in your Network Plan, you might need to rethink and change your Career Plan.   Make sense? We will discuss this further in the chapter entitled "The Network Plan."

Whew, that was a long section!   We discussed how to create a gap list, how to use that gap list to identify potential jobs that will close skill and experience gaps, and how to leverage your Career Plan in different situations. We hinted at the connection between your Career Plan and your Network Plan.   In the next chapter we're going to explain the Network Plan, how to build it and how to use it to improve your chances of realizing your goals.   Excited? Me too!   So let's get to it!

Section 3: The Network Plan

Chapter 16: Why Do You Need a Network Plan?

Now that you have a Career Plan, it's a simple matter of implementation. Well, it isn't quite that simple. Just by virtue of having a Career Plan, you will be better equipped to compete than your peers, that's for sure. The odds will be in your favor, but how can you improve your odds even more? The answer is the Network Plan. In this section I'll explain the importance of networks and the different kinds of networks that may be useful to you. We'll discuss why working hard isn't good enough and why remaining visible is critical. And finally, I'll explain how the Network Plan will reduce stress levels by creating targeted opportunities.

This may seem a little off the topic, but bear with me please. Have you ever wondered how companies turn their products into household names? I mean, how do you take something as mundane and personal as toilet paper and create a name that nearly everyone can recognize? Those of you in your 50s will remember, "Charmin, it doesn't feel like toilet paper[1]." Do you remember the commercials?   Can you still see Mr. Whipple reprimanding the shoppers for squeezing the toilet paper because it's so irresistibly soft, and then getting caught doing the same?   How about this one: "Nationwide is on your side[2]."   I bet you sang the jingle in your head as you read that, didn't you!   How did they get these images, phrases and songs so deeply ingrained into our memory? The answer is simple.... marketing.

According to Wikipedia, "marketing is the process of communicating the value of a product or service to customers for the purpose of selling the product or service. It is a critical business function for attracting customers." It is through the process of marketing that companies make people aware of a good product and make people <u>want</u> and even <u>need</u> that product.   It is marketing that keeps a product in front of people to remind them the product exists and that they need it, thereby never taking the chance that people might forget the product exists. Marketing is essential for a company's survival.   And I believe it is essential in managing your career!

Let's look at it this way.   What if you were a corporation and you wanted to sell your product and make

---

[1] Charmin toilet paper. Advertisement. 1960's. Television.
[2] Nationwide jingle. Advertisement. Multiple years. Television.

your company as successful as possible. What would you do?

First, you would have to identify the product. In Career Management, you have one, and only one, product to market — **YOU**. Next, you would assess the quality of your product, identify any deficiencies, and then make the necessary improvements to make your product competitive in the marketplace. You did that in the Career Planning section when you created your Career Plan, didn't you? You assessed your skills and experiences, determined the skills and experiences required to compete for the job(s) you wanted, and then created a skill and experience gap list. Then you created a plan to close those gaps. The next step is to create a marketing plan outlining your target market (i.e. who's going to buy your product). This is where your Network Plan comes into play. We'll talk about that more in a bit. Finally, you would create a communication plan aimed at making people aware of the quality of your product and making them *want* and *need* you on their team. We did some of this by creating a resume that shows career growth and accomplishments. We'll do more by leveraging your Network Plan.

Honestly, there is one more step. The *real* final step is to have a plan to keep your product in the front of people's minds so they don't forget your product exists. Let me give you an example to show why staying visible is so important. I worked for IBM for 29 years. Early in my career I progressed quickly into a management position, leading a team of programmers. I was part of the "up and coming" group that management was grooming for bigger and better things. Our location was growing and we eventually outgrew our building. Management decided to move part of the population to some buildings we rented on the other side of town about 10 miles away. My team was part of the group that moved. I spent every day with my head down, working hard to achieve my objectives and continue to move up the corporate ladder. About six months had gone by when I happened to be close to the main location, so I decided to stop in for lunch. As I was walking down the hall I bumped into one of the members of the senior management team, a person I knew very well. We both said hello and chit-chatted for a minute. But then he said something that changed my life. He said, "Where ya been?" I was young and I admit, I didn't know what he meant so I responded like most people would. I said, "I've been on the other side of town; you moved me over there, remember?" Again he said, "I know, but *where have you been*? I forgot you work here. You should make it a priority to be at the main location at least once a week so senior management remembers you work here. The site manager is looking for someone to solve a problem for him right now! It's a problem you are perfectly suited for but your name hasn't popped into his head." I was floored. It hit me like a ton of bricks. I'm missing career opportunities, not because I'm not working hard and achieving my objectives, but because my name and my capabilities have been pushed into the deep, dark recesses of our senior manager's mind!   He forgot about me. From that point on I never went more than a week without making a planned appearance at the main site.   I planned where I would be and who I wanted to "bump into" every time I went to the site.   Opportunities began to come my way again.

That example was the foundation of my thoughts around networking.   The design and implementation of the Network Plan was born about 15 years later when I was managing an account for one of IBM's Information Technology outsourcing deals.   I was in a meeting with the marketing team working on a plan to sell IBM products in the account.   We discussed key customer contacts and labeled those who would make the buying decision versus those who couldn't make a buying decision but were key influencers for the buyers.   We noted who on our team had a relationship with each key customer contact and documented the kind of relationship, meaning was it a personal relationship extending beyond work, did the two work side-by-side with no outside relationship, etc.   Once we understood who the key people were and how we knew them, we developed an action plan to leverage each relationship to market our products and build momentum to buy.   When we were finished I realized the same approach could be used for career management. With a good marketing plan, a person can create and manage the relationships that are key to realizing their career goals. This experience gave me the framework I needed to create the Network Plan that I will teach you in the next two chapters.

The important thing to remember is, **<u>YOU</u>** are your only product. The success of your company (your family) depends on how well you market and sell your product. No one cares about you and your family more than you! This entire book is dedicated to teaching you how to market yourself the <u>RIGHT Way</u>, at the <u>RIGHT Time</u>, to the <u>RIGHT People</u>. Are you ready to do some marketing? Good! Then let's get to it…

I work really hard. I come in early. I stay late. My boss knows how hard I work and I'm always getting compliments on the quality of my work. But I can't seem to get ahead. I work for people who used to report to me. I'm better than they are; that should be me in that management position, getting the big bucks. I guess it's all about <u>who you know</u>, not <u>what you know</u>… Have you ever heard this story? Truth be told, I'm tired of hearing it. That's partly why I'm writing this book. People, listen please — doing good work is very important. <u>It is table stakes</u>. True enough, even a bad product can have some success, but it will be short-lived. People eventually realize the product is limited and the marketing may have been misleading. If you don't do your job and do it well, you cannot compete and will not realize your long-term career goals. But that's where it ends. As you progress through the early phases of your career, you will realize that everyone works hard and is good at what they do. That's what I mean by table stakes. Working hard and doing quality work gets you on an even playing field with everyone else. But if that's true, how do you get ahead? By creating and properly using your Network Plan. It is "who you know," but not in the sense of our chronic complainer above. I would say it's more like "who you know that can help you get ahead." People with limited skills and experience cannot get ahead purely based on who they know. Again, they might get a break or two, but that's where it ends. But think about it this way — when you want to get a new roof for your house, you might open up the phone book and pick a roofer based on their ad. You don't want to pick someone from an ad, but you might have to if you don't know anything about the roofers available to you. But if you know people who can provide a good recommendation, you're more likely to select the roofer they suggest, aren't you? Even better, you'll pick the roofer with whom you have had a positive experience, the one you already know and trust to do a good job. Of course you would. And the same is true in business. When I'm looking for someone to fill a position on my team, I want to pick a known quantity. I want someone whose character, attitude, quality of work, and work ethic are already known to me. If I don't know any of the candidates I will rely on recommendations from people I trust, or more clearly, people who are in a position of influence with me. I will not pick someone from a "ready now" list. I'd rather leave the position open. So you see, doing good work really is just table stakes.

Earlier I said it isn't "who you know," but it's more like "who you know who can help you get ahead." I'd like to simplify that thought a bit. It isn't "who you know," but it is "who knows what you can do for them!" Hiring managers will select a known quantity over an unknown quantity almost every time. That's not to say the hiring of a friend will never happen. But more often than not, the hiring manager will hire someone known to him (or a trusted advisor), someone who he knows has the drive, attitude and work ethic he is looking for to make his life easier. He will hire someone he already knows can do the job, not someone from a "ready now" list. Marketing yourself, making contacts, making sure people <u>know who you are and what you are capable of doing</u> is what allows you to compete and win.

Hopefully you agree that networking is a key component of career management. There are literally dozens and dozens of potential networks that will help you in your career. We're going to explore the network within your company in the next two chapters so I'll skip that for now.   The networks outside of your company are equally important, especially if your Career Plan includes a move outside of your current company. The internet is a great tool to find networks.   Different professional groups are abundant and have active chapters in just about every large city.   Get involved. Make an effort to meet people and share information. Make connections, take notes and help each other create opportunities.   Join the social networking site LinkedIn.   They do a great job of connecting people with similar interests and providing the opportunity to expand your network into a larger geography.

A Network Plan is essential for marketing yourself and for creating career opportunities.   Let's move on to the next chapter where I will describe the components of the plan. Then we'll talk about how to fill out your personal Network Plan.

Chapter 17: The Components

There are nine data elements in the Network Plan. Each data element is designed to identify the people who can help you achieve your goals, the role they play, and the Action Plan you will implement to create or nurture your relationships. When we finish this chapter you will understand each data element in the Network Plan, and you will be ready to discuss how to populate and leverage your plan to create opportunities, compete for jobs, and increase your chances of winning!

Figure 9: The Network Plan on page 91 provides a visual representation of the Network Plan. It is designed as a table for ease of maintenance. Each row represents a relationship while the columns represent key data points about the relationship. The columns are arranged in such a way as to support the thought process required when filling out a row. Okay, let's get to it!

Personal Network Plan

Name	Role	Relationship	Decision Maker Influencer	Supporter Neutral Detractor	Advocate Yes / No	Goal State Marketing Plan	Action Plan	Focus Priority

This is a **PRIVATE** document and should not be shared with anyone!

FIGURE 9: THE NETWORK PLAN

NAME

In this column you list the names of everyone that requires your attention to develop a new relationship, rekindle an existing relationship, or to repair a broken one. It sounds like this might be an awful lot of people, and it could be. So how does one determine who should go on their Network Plan? Use the Career Plan! The reason I recommend building the Career Plan first is to:

1. Foster thinking about what you enjoy doing every day to help identify career goals
2. Help with the identification of the RIGHT People to add to your Network Plan

Look at your Career Plan and think about the people who can help you achieve each step in the plan. If a person is a hiring manager for a position in your Career Plan, add the name to your Network Plan. If the person has a relationship with a hiring manager and that hiring manager values their opinion, add the name to your Network Plan. If the person holds the position you want, add the name to your Network Plan. At this point you shouldn't worry about adding 30, 40, or even 50 or more names to your list. We'll pare them down in a minute. For now, just be sure you identify everyone that could play a role in helping you achieve your career goals.

ROLE

Describe the role the person plays in the organization. You can keep it really simple and list their official title. Or you can add a few words describing the role they play. For example, you can put VP, Corporate Applications as someone's role. What if this VP has a close relationship with and is a trusted advisor of the Enterprise CIO and the Executive VP of Human Resources? If one of your goals is to become VP, Human Resources, wouldn't you want to note that in your Network Plan? Do you see the difference between someone's official title and the role they play in the organization? I'm not suggesting you spend hours researching and thinking about every individual on your list. But I am suggesting you consider key relationships or leverage points when listing someone's role and decide if their role in the organization warrants noting in your plan.

RELATIONSHIP

In this section I want you to list how you know the person. To put it a different way, briefly describe your current relationship. I'm not looking for a book here. I'm basically looking for you to write down how you know the person and what existing opportunities you have to make contact with him. For example, did you work for him in a previous job? Did he work for you? Were you colleagues working side-by-side? Do you have a personal relationship outside of work?   For example, do your kids play on the same soccer team?   Do you go to the same church?   Do you support the same charities and spend time at fundraisers together?

Make sense?   Basically I want you to list how you know the person and identify your interaction opportunities so we can put them to good use when we create your Action Plan.

DECISION MAKER / INFLUENCER

This column seems pretty straightforward, and it is. Simply note in your Network Plan if the person is the one who will make the hiring decision for one of your goal jobs or is a person of influence for the hiring manager. Obviously you have to think about a particular step in your Career Plan to make the Decision Maker / Influencer assessment.   Therein lies the complicating factor: a person can be a Decision Maker for one of your goals and an Influencer for another.   So how do you decide which descriptor to use?   The answer is, it depends.   Don't you hate that answer?   I do, but in this case it's true.   I want to introduce the concept that your Network Plan will be a living document.   It will change as you think about each job opportunity in your Career Plan.   For example, if you look at a lateral move, the person on your plan might be the hiring manager and therefore listed as a Decision Maker.   But if you're considering a promotional opportunity, that same person might be a trusted advisor of the hiring manager and you would list him as an Influencer.

I know what's running through your mind. You're thinking the Network Plan will grow out of control and become unwieldy very quickly. Yup, it could. But it shouldn't if you use it correctly. You can list a person as both a Decision Maker and an Influencer in your plan, depending on the Career Plan opportunity. If you choose to do this, you just need to note the opportunity for which the person is a Decision Maker. I suggest noting where the person is a Decision Maker because it is likely that the person will be an Influencer more often than a decision maker.

SUPPORTER / NEUTRAL / DETRACTOR

At this point the next question is about what the person thinks about you. Is the person a supporter of yours, meaning does he know your skills and experiences? Does the person have an active relationship with you and does he clearly understand the value you can bring to the organization? Is your only experience with the person a project that went horribly wrong? If you've never met the person, do you think they know who you are based on your reputation or from their interactions with influencers? The answers to these questions will determine how you should fill out this column. Contrary to the Decision

Maker / Influencer question where the answer depends on the job you are currently considering, the answer here is an absolute. Either the person knows you or they don't. Remember, it isn't about you knowing them, <u>it's about them knowing you</u>!

Let's briefly describe each category…

<u>Supporter:</u>
A Supporter is a person who knows you well. A Supporter knows your skills and experiences, understands the value you bring to the company, and believes you have the ability to bring even more value to the company in the future. Clearly, you've had a previous relationship where your skills and experiences were on display. A Supporter is aware of your reputation and has likely contributed to it.

<u>Neutral:</u>
If you filled out the Relationship column and noted that you have little to no relationship with the person, you should call them "Neutral" in terms of their support for you. Neutral isn't all bad. It just means in your opinion the person doesn't know you well enough to be a Supporter. He isn't aware of your skills and experiences and doesn't realize your true value. Not yet that is! But hey, at least he isn't a Detractor!

Another possibility is that the person knows you but may not be aware of your full breadth of skills and experiences. For example, he may have worked with you early in your career, and you may even be fairly good friends. But even good friends lose touch sometimes. He may not have worked with you for years, and may not know how your career has progressed.

Detractor:

Similar to a Supporter, a Detractor is also a person who knows you well, knows your skills and experiences and understands the value you bring to the company. However, in this case the Detractor believes your skills and experiences are seriously lacking in what it takes to be successful.   A Detractor doesn't believe you have the skills and experiences to take on a higher level job and provide value to the company.   In short, a Detractor will actively try to be sure someone else he believes is more capable gets the job rather than you.   I'm not implying a Detractor is a person who is out to "get you."   What I'm saying is a Detractor is a person who doesn't believe you have the skills and experiences to compete at the level at which you are trying to compete.

Obviously you want as many Supporters on your list as possible. But the most important aspect of this exercise is to include the <u>RIGHT People</u> and categorize people correctly. It does you no good to categorize incorrectly so you can feel good about yourself. Calling a Neutral person a Supporter will result in the wrong Action Plan and a wasted relationship opportunity. Categorizing a Detractor as Neutral will leave a negative person out in the organization, actively working against you. I can't stress enough how important it is to categorize people correctly. Most of the time you'll have a good idea of where to place people based on past relationships, conversations you've had with other people or any number of other ways. When you don't, it's imperative that you leverage mentors, friends and colleagues to form an opinion. In fact, even if you believe a person is a Supporter, I recommend you test your theory, just to be sure.

ADVOCATE (YES / NO) ?

This column is a subcategory for the Supporter designation. The question is, "If you have a Supporter on your list, is the person an Advocate or not?" In other words, will the person pick up the phone and call the hiring manager to provide important information about you and explain why you are perfect for the job? Or will she support you to your face but decline to take any action to help you? Will your Supporter argue on your behalf in the meeting where the final candidates are discussed? Or will she let the conversation play out because it isn't politically correct to go against the crowd? Do you have a Supporter who is an Advocate, or do you have a "closet" Supporter? It's important to understand the kind of

Supporter you have so you can craft the appropriate Action Plan to turn your closet Supporters into Advocates!

GOAL STATE / MARKETING PLAN

At this point you should know where each person in your Network Plan stands.   Now you need to determine where you want them to be.   That's the purpose of the Goal State / Marketing Plan.   In this column you will document the answer, or the end result, of your efforts with each individual person.   For example, if you have a Supporter who is an Advocate already, perhaps your goal is simply to make your relationship more active by meeting with that person at least once a quarter. Remember, avoid "where ya been" situations! Maybe you have a Detractor and your goal is to move the Detractor into a Neutral position.   Or if you've determined a Detractor cannot be moved to a position of Neutral, maybe you simply want to minimize the damage the Detractor can do.

The Goal State / Marketing Plan is the section where you will document what relationship you want from each person.   It describes the ultimate goal you expect to achieve after implementing your Action Plan.   I crafted the order of the Network Plan very carefully.   I want you to understand where each person currently sits, understand where you want them to be (the answer or Goal State) and then craft an Action Plan to make your Goal State a reality.

ACTION PLAN

The Action Plan is the most critical aspect of the Network Plan. Here you will document the actions you will take to create new relationships, improve existing relationships, and increase the breadth and depth of what people know about you, all in support of your desire to give yourself the best possible chance to compete.

Your Action Plan will be influenced by your current assessments and Goal State / Marketing Plan. It can include various activities spanning from in-depth career conversations to the development of new relationships. The key point is all activities should be aimed solely at creating or improving your relationships (i.e. your Network) and ensuring the RIGHT People know you and the value you can bring to the organization and to them!

FOCUS PRIORITY

When we discussed the "Name" column I told you to list as many names as you need, but to be sure to list everyone who could play a role in helping you achieve your goals. I don't care if you have 50 names on your list. Just be sure to list everyone. So how do you manage a large list of names? If you try to actively manage 50 relationships, you won't have time to do your job and things will quickly unravel. The purpose of the Focus Priority column is to rank the urgency required when managing a relationship. For example, a person who will play a key role in the next potential opportunity as described in your Career Plan will be ranked as a 1, or very high Focus Priority. You need their help and you need it in the near future. On the other end of the spectrum you might have a person who will play a key role for an opportunity that you hope to have in five years. It is important to begin your work in creating a relationship with this person, but the extent of your activity in the short-term will be far less than it will be when the opportunity draws closer. In this case you may give this Action Plan a Focus Priority of 10 signifying that you will do minimal work on this relationship. Make sense?

I recommend having no more than 5 to 7 people with the highest Focus Priority. You manage your Network Plan while doing your job and you simply can't actively manage more than a handful of people and still do your work well. Never lose focus on doing the best you can do every day.   Remember, good performance is "table stakes."

That's it for the Network Plan, folks. You should have a good understanding of all the elements of the Network Plan, how to populate each column and how to create Action Plans that move you towards your Goal State job(s). In the next chapter we're going to discuss how to take the Network Plan you just created and leverage it to ensure you're focusing on the <u>RIGHT People</u> at the <u>RIGHT Time</u> to give yourself the best chance of competing and thereby the best chance of winning!

Chapter 18: How Do You Use Your Network Plan?

At this point you should understand why you need a Network Plan, and you should have at least a cursory understanding of each component and how to use it.   In this chapter we're going to explore how to use your Network Plan to your advantage. We're going to tie <u>your</u> Career Plan to <u>your</u> Network Plan in a way that brings Career Management into greater focus. Are you ready? Good, let's get started.

All through this book, we've been talking about things we need to do and documents we need to create to share with others. We want to ensure our career goals are understood and hiring managers know who we are and what we are capable of doing for them.   I am a big believer in sharing your career goals and your personal capabilities with people. However, the one exception is the Network Plan.   This plan contains a list of people with whom you need to develop or manage a relationship. While there is nothing wrong with writing a few things down to help organize your thoughts and actions, people on the list may not like seeing their name written down next to an Action Plan.   This document could be misinterpreted as an attempt to manipulate a person's perception rather than a document to help you create and manage relationships. You need to understand and feel good about the purpose of your Network Plan. It is not a plan to manipulate people. I cannot stress this enough. **The Network Plan is a plan to provide information to the <u>RIGHT People</u>, at the <u>RIGHT Time,</u> to ensure they know you, know what you can do for them, and remember you when they need help**. You have to be clear about this point in your own mind and you have to use this document as it is intended. If you don't have the necessary table stakes and you use this document to manipulate people, it will backfire on you. People will eventually figure out what's happening and your career will be over, at least at your current company. The Network Plan is a very powerful tool to ensure your capabilities and your ability to help are known by the <u>RIGHT People</u>, at the <u>RIGHT Time</u>. Use it the <u>RIGHT Way</u> and it will improve your ability to compete and improve the odds that you will achieve your career goals.

<u>What's in a Name?</u>

In an earlier chapter we discussed how to leverage the Career Plan to populate the Network Plan. We said to include hiring managers, close advisors, and even people who are currently in a position you want. This is a great start to populate your plan. Is that all? Are there any other people you might want to include? I think there are other potential additions to consider. In your personal situation you may or may not want to include these people. It's entirely up to you. All I suggest is that you consider them and make a conscious decision about each one.

Executive Management Teams

In some companies, executive management teams control hiring decisions, especially new executive hiring decisions. Even if they don't control them they are heavy Influencers. It makes sense if you think about it — executive teams need to be cohesive, high-performing groups of individuals. Notice I didn't say they had to be of a single mind. Different opinions often are a team strength if the team is cohesive and high-performing, meaning the team can have a direct, heated conversation without letting the conversation become personal. The team appreciates being challenged and understands that the ensuing dialogue will lead to the best decision. Also note that I said executive teams are made up of individual people. You already know that your Network Plan should include an executive who is in direct line of sight of a job in your Career Plan. But what about the rest of the executive team? The answer is, maybe... In some organizations the senior management team will discuss all new executive hires to be sure the person will fit into the current team. It isn't a question of fitting into a mold, but rather a question of what the person brings to the team. Will the person fill a gap in the executive team? Will she make the team stronger? Or will she create a rift amongst the team? It might make sense for you to include the entire executive team in your Network Plan, especially if you are going after an executive position. But you don't have to be best buds with everyone. Your goal is simply to make sure they understand you would be a valuable addition to the executive team.

If you work in a large corporation, I'm sure you're wondering how you can get to know several hundred, or maybe even several thousand executives. That's not practical and not what I'm saying. If you work in IT you might need to know the CIO team of executives. Or maybe you work in a particular product line and you want to move up in that same area. Then you need to know that executive team. If you want to move to another part of the business you need to know those executives. Get the point? Focus your Network Plan on the areas you need for your current Career Plan timeframe.

External Organizations / Contacts

Most of this book has been focused on the company you work for right now and the people within your company. External contacts can be equally important! For example, most senior executives are on external boards of charities, churches, other companies, etc. Why not you? I can't think of a better way to develop a relationship with a senior executive than to work side by side with her at the community food bank. Joining an external organization can be helpful too.   Executives, managers and peers (future hiring managers?) belong to external groups.   Search the internet for "professional organizations" in your city and you will find dozens of groups where you can learn and make important network connections. You can build a lot of relationships and identify additional people for your Network Plan simply by joining and attending their meetings.

The plan is so big! How do You know where to start?

Your Network Plan could be pretty big at this point. You might have 30, 40 or even 100 names on it. How do you sort through it all? Remember what we said earlier. Use the Focus Priority to identify the 5 to 7 people that are the most critical for you right now and go actively implement your Action Plan for each one.   Once you have these plans moving, identify the next most important group of people.   This might be a group that will be influential in the second career step in your plan.   You might want to create an Action Plan for this group that prepares your relationships for the time when they move into the top priority group.   It might be as simple as introducing yourself to someone who doesn't know you.   Or requesting a mentor relationship with someone.   Think about it. If you put a case together explaining why you want to mentor with an executive, even if the answer is "no, I'm too busy" that executive will know more about you than he did before your request, right? Again, it isn't that you now know him. It's that he knows more about you and what you are capable of because you told him about yourself in your request.

To net it out, use your Career Plan to organize your Network Plan. Be more aggressive with short-term career moves vs long-term moves. And don't be afraid to leave the Action Plan blank for some people. As you review and manage your Network Plan, Action Plans will change as well as your Focus Priorities. Relationships will grow and you will need to alter the description of how you know someone. The point is, things change over time. Build your Network Plan for today and the near-term future, and use it. If you don't think it's quite right, no worries. You're going to change it in a few months anyway.

Let's look at a few example activities you might include in your Network Plan...

Supporter:
If you have a Supporter who is also an Advocate, your Goal State for the person may be to keep them as an Advocate. So your Action Plan may be as simple as having lunch once a month to keep your relationship active. The appropriate timeframe depends on how well you know the person. Don't let geography become an

excuse.   A phone call to ask about the family will work too!   If your Supporter isn't an Advocate and your Goal State is to get him there, you would have activities geared towards improving his knowledge of your skills and experiences.   It is possible your Supporter isn't an Advocate due to political reasons.   For example, maybe he is on thin ice with the big boss at the moment.   It is important to understand your Supporter's situation before investing too much time trying to move him to an Advocate.   If you determine the time isn't right and the stars just aren't aligned for it, wait for the <u>RIGHT Time</u> to take action to move your Supporter to an Advocate.

<u>Neutral:</u>

With a Neutral person your Action Plan will be focused on creating or developing a relationship with them. Remember, a Neutral person likely doesn't know you, or perhaps has met you but doesn't know much about you. You need to fix that problem.   Regardless of your Goal State, your primary goal will be to ensure the Neutral person doesn't slip back into a Detractor role.   Once you're sure they won't become a Detractor, you need to assess the reason why this person is a Neutral.   If it's because of a lack of information, your Action Plan will be geared towards providing information.   If it's because they don't know you at all, your Action Plan will be geared towards an introduction and the creation of a relationship.

Detractor:

Hopefully you won't have any Detractors in your Network Plan. But if you do, you need to create a thoughtful Action Plan for each of them. The worst thing you can do is ignore a Detractor. Detractors can cause irreparable damage to your Career Plan, especially if the Detractor is in a position of influence at high levels in the organization. Goal States can vary widely for Detractors and range from neutralizing their ability to influence to moving them to at least a Neutral position. Possible Action Plan activities to neutralize a Detractor can include enlisting your Supporters to counterbalance the Detractor's opinion or creating stronger relationships with the hiring manager and his influencers to minimize the Detractor's influence. Moving a Detractor to a position of Neutral will follow many of the same activities employed to move a Neutral person to a Supporter and a Supporter to an Advocate.

Conclusion

Well folks, we've come to the end of the book. In the chapter on resume writing, we discussed the chronological style and why managers prefer that type of resume. We outlined the content and dove into the detail of each section. And finally, we examined some resume "dos and don'ts" for your awareness.

In the next chapter, we moved on to the Career Plan. I showed you how to assess your skills and experiences and, more importantly, how to determine what other people think about your skills and experiences. We discussed how to figure out where you are, where you want to be, and how to map out the steps to get there.

And finally, we built a Network Plan. We defined the components of the Network Plan and how to fill out each part. We considered who should be in your Network Plan and how you can use your plan to position yourself to compete for jobs. And finally we explored how the Career Plan and the Network Plan work together and complement each other.

Each individual component is valuable. Now that you've read this book, you should understand how they can be used together to create the opportunities you want and need to realize your career goals.

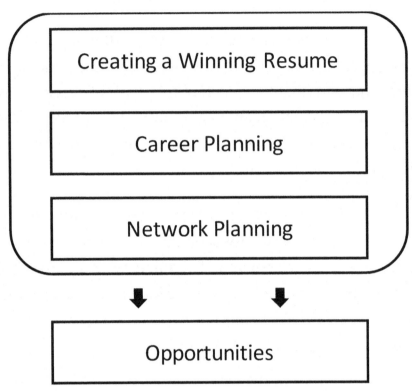

FIGURE 10: THE CAREER MANAGEMENT PROCESS

As you've probably noticed by now, I am not your typical executive. I know how to manage my way through large company politics, but I don't play games. I don't have an "agenda" and I don't take sides. I am a straight-shooter. I tell the truth and I always try to do what I believe is right, based on what I know at that moment in time. When I managed outsourcing accounts for IBM, I had the mindset that I worked for my customer, not IBM.

I tried to do what was right for my customer, so they could be successful. I created a vision and a mindset on my team to think the same way. I only mention this to provide additional context for the messages in this book. I've tried to convey how managers operate and how they perceive information when working through the hiring process. I laid it out in the simplest and most straightforward terms, with no BS. I tried to take 36 years of experience with managers from multiple companies in various industries and boil it down to give you insight into how managers think and consume information, along with some practical steps you can take to take control of your career. I've consolidated some key points from our discussion into a "Career Management Top 10 List" on page 114 to help you keep the most important messages in the front of your mind. Whenever you feel like you're losing energy behind your efforts, pull out the list and read through it.

Career Management Top 10 List	
10)	Your Career Plan is going to happen **with or without your involvement**
9)	Eliminate your "where ya beens"
8)	Go after your targeted opportunities that will help you achieve your goal
7)	You have to create and nurture opportunities
6)	Revisit your plan on an annual basis
5)	It's okay to make changes to your plan. It's okay to take a career break.
4)	It's about who knows you and what you can do for them
3)	Compete ≠ Win
2)	No one cares about you, your family or your career more than you do
1)	Invest in yourself. You are worth it!

FIGURE 11: CAREER MANAGEMENT TOP 10 LIST

You have to work hard to manage your career; there's no way around it. I hope this book has helped you understand that by planning your career and working hard at creating a network of support, you will improve your ability to compete and you will feel more in control of your career. I wish you the best of luck and great success as you market yourself the <u>RIGHT Way</u>, at the <u>RIGHT Time</u>, to the <u>RIGHT People</u>!

Appendices: Key Graphics

Appendix A: Career Management Process

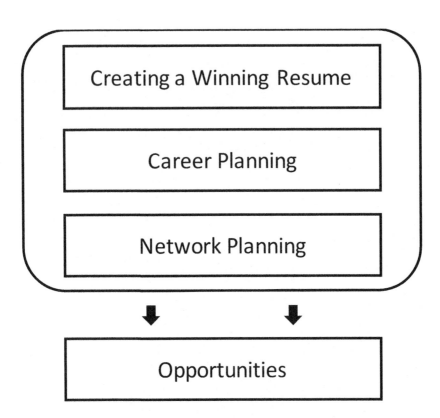

Appendix B: Components of a Resume

The Resume

Overview

Job History

Job Description

Accomplishments

⬇   ⬇

Job Description

Accomplishments

Miscellaneous

The Career Planning Process

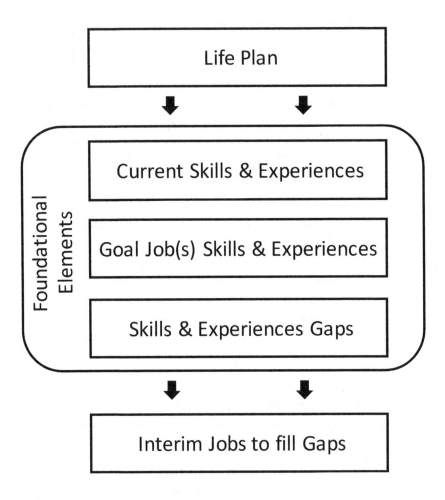

Appendix D: Sample Career Plan

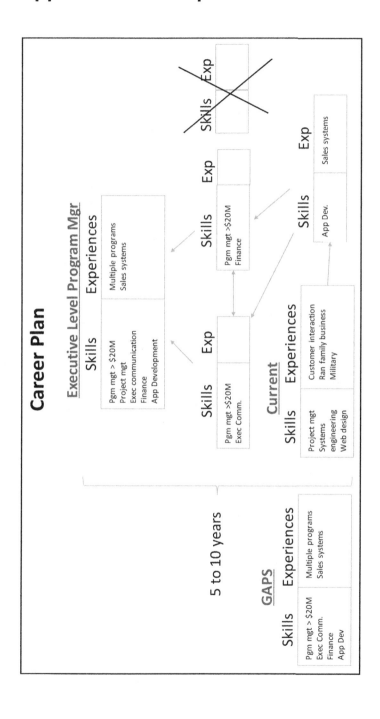

Appendix E: Network Plan

Personal Network Plan

Name	Role	Relationship	Decision Maker Influencer	Supporter Neutral Detractor	Advocate Yes / No	Goal State Marketing Plan	Action Plan	Focus Priority

This is a **PRIVATE** document and should not be shared with anyone!

Appendix F: Top 10 list

Career Management Top 10 List

10)   Your Career Plan is going to happen **with or without your involvement**

9)   Eliminate your "where ya beens"

8)   Go after your targeted opportunities that will help you achieve your goal

7)   You have to create and nurture opportunities

6)   Revisit your plan on an annual basis

5)   It's okay to make changes to your plan. It's okay to take a career break.

4)   It's about who knows you and what you can do for them

3)   Compete ≠ Win

2)   No one cares about you, your family or your career more than you do

1)   Invest in yourself. You are worth it!

ABOUT THE AUTHOR

Ray Hoppenjans is a former executive with IBM and Nationwide Insurance and has over 30 years of management experience in various industries. While at IBM, Ray managed outsourcing accounts with multiple IBM customers including Eastman Kodak, Hertz, ACE Insurance, Lincoln Financial, Allianz Life and more. His daily interactions with customer executives and managers laid the foundation for his approach to coaching and career management. Ray used his experience to develop a practical approach that outlines how executives and hiring managers evaluate, hire and promote people. Using his approach, he has helped hundreds of people advance in their careers. People who have used his approach feel confident and more in control of their own destiny. He is currently retired and lives in Vonore, Tennessee.

Ray is available to present to groups or provide individual consulting. He is developing a workbook complete with multiple fillable worksheets, self-reflection prompts, and exercises to help you achieve your career goal.

Check out "TheProductIsYouConsulting.com" for additional detail.

Made in the USA
Coppell, TX
27 January 2020